AFFiRM KiDS

Consuelo Gaines

AFFIRM KIDS
Affirm Series Volume III

Consuelo Gaines
cgaineskdg@gmail.com

ISBN 978-1-949826-64-7

Printed in the USA.

Published by: EAGLES GLOBAL PUBLISHING | Frisco, Texas
In conjunction with the 2023 Eagles Authors Course
Cover & interior designed by DestinedToPublish.com

DEDICATION

This work is dedicated to Kingdom kids, globally. May you grow in grace – multiplied blessings of agape and shalom - knowing that your true identity, destiny, and success are found in Christ alone!

iv

NOTE FROM THE AUTHOR

It is my prayer that this volume will motivate, inspire, encourage, and empower you. May the affirmations draw us ever closer to Father God through His Word and through the Living Word, Jesus, into the greatness and success God has planned for each one of His children.

CONTENTS

SECTION
Introduction

INTRODUCTION

Greetings Families And Friends,

Welcome to the Affirm For Kids Volume of the Affirm to Realize Series. This is the third volume following the adult titles: <u>Affirm Greatness Realize Destiny</u> and <u>Affirm Greatness Realize Success</u>. As in the first two adult volumes, the pages that follow are guides to focusing our thoughts, words, and actions on what God says about us in the Bible.

The world around us is often full of negative messages that cause us to believe, think, and act out things that are opposite of what God says about us in the Bible. If you are a Christian, it is important to be, believe, act, and think like Jesus. It is my prayer that this tool will help youth, and everyone, to do this in an easy and simple yet impactful way.

While the book is written to be friendly to younger ages, it is a tool that can be used for everyone.

Author, Consuelo Gaines

WAYS TO USE THIS BOOK

This book is designed to be used in multiple ways to suit the reader's and family's needs. Some ways in which it can be used include are as:

- A stand-alone kids' devotional with scriptures and affirmations to read, speak, and memorize

- An emergent readers' devotional to repeat scriptures and affirmations in echo form

- A companion kid devotional to the adult volumes of the Affirm to Realize series for family devotions

- A month long kid devotional

- A weekly youth devotional using a section each week for four weeks

- Your own customized devotional

Youth can also create and add their own affirmations to the devotional. Youth can use journals as companions to their daily affirmations drawing or writing thoughts about the affirmations and scriptures.

Whatever way you and your family decide to use this book, the tools here are to empower readers to know, think, speak, and act upon what God says about us. The truths of Scripture are timeless and for us all. So read them, repeat them often, memorize them, rehearse them, meditate on them, and add to them by creating your own.

Use this book over and over to remind yourself who you are in God and what God says and thinks about us. Believing, knowing, and doing these things will grow us into who God has chosen us to be, leading us into our destiny and into success!

SECTION
One

I AM CREATED BY GOD!

GOD MADE ME SPECIAL LIKE HIM!

God created me and made me special.

"Then God said, 'Let us make human beings in our image and likeness. And let them rule over the fish in the sea and the birds in the sky. Let them rule over the tame animals, over all the earth and over all the small crawling animals on the earth.'"
Genesis 1:26 (ICB)

GOD MADE ME HIS MASTERPIECE!

"God has made us what we are. In Christ Jesus, God made us new people so that we would do good works. God had planned in advance those good works for us. He had planned for us to live our lives doing them."
Ephesians 2:10 (ICB)

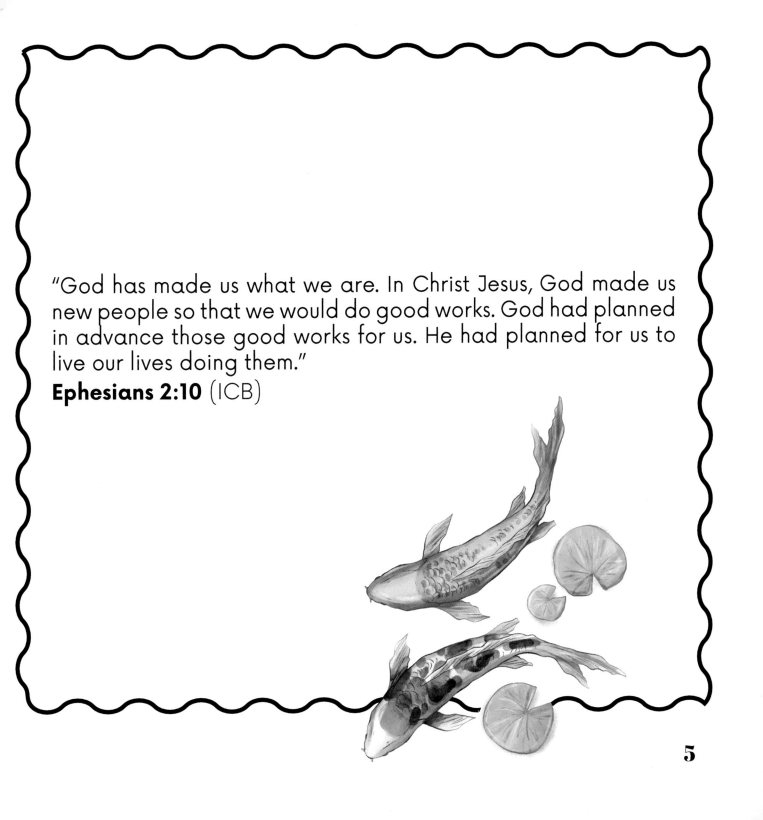

GOD MADE ME WONDERFUL!

I AM CREATED WONDERFULLY!

"I praise you because you made me in an amazing and wonderful way. What you have done is wonderful. I know this very well."
Psalm 139:14 (ICB)

GOD PAYS SPECIAL ATTENTION TO ME!

GOD CROWNS ME WITH GLORY
GOD CROWNS ME WITH HONOR

"You made man[kind] a little lower than the angels. And you crowned [them] with glory and honor."
Psalm 8:5 (ICB)

GOD MADE ME A
BOSS TO RULE
LIKE HIM!

"You put him in charge of everything you made. You put all things under his control."
Psalm 8:6 (ICB)

GOD MADE
ME HIS!

I BELONG
TO HIM!

I AM GOD'S SPECIAL POSSESSION.

"Now this is what the Lord says. He created you, people of Jacob. He formed you, people of Israel. He says, 'Don't be afraid, because I have saved you. I have called you by name, and you are mine.'"
Isaiah 43:1 (ICB)

GOD MADE ME FOR HIS PLEASURE!

"Our Lord and God! You are worthy to receive glory and honor and power. You made all things. Everything existed and was made because you wanted it."
Revelation 4:11 (ICB)

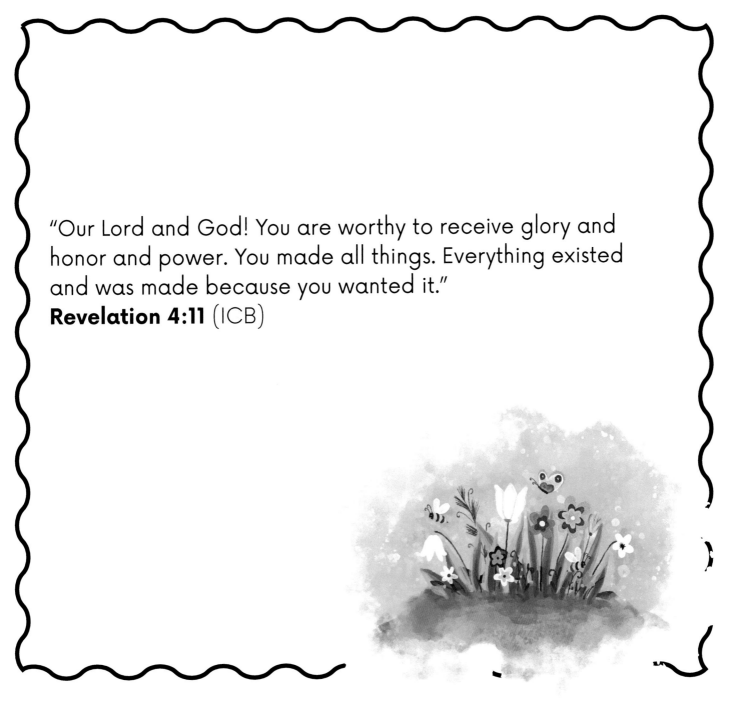

I AM CREATED BY GOD!

SECTION
two

I AM LOVED BY GOD

GOD LOVES ME!

GOD LOVES US ALL

"For God loved the world so much that he gave his only Son. God gave his Son so that whoever believes in him may not be lost, but have eternal life."
John 3:16 (ICB)

GOD SHOWS HIS LOVE FOR US IN ACTIONS

- God became human like us through Jesus.
- Jesus showed us how to live pleasing to God.
- Jesus died to take our place and free us from sin.

"Christ died for us while we were still sinners. In this way God showed his great love for us."
Romans 8:5 (ICB)

NOTHING CAN COME BETWEEN ME AND GOD

"Yes, I am sure that nothing can separate us from the love God has for us. Not death, not life, not angels, not ruling spirits, nothing now, nothing in the future, no powers, nothing above us, nothing below us, or anything else in the whole world will ever be able to separate us from the love of God that is in Christ Jesus our Lord."

Romans 8:38 (ICB)

GOD'S LOVE FOR ME IS GREAT!

GOD LOVES ME MORE THAN ANY OTHER.

"The Father has loved us so much! He loved us so much that we are called children of God."
1 John 3:1a (ICB)

GOD LOVES ME FIRST!

"True love is God's love for us, not our love for God. God sent his Son to die in our place to take away our sins."
1 John 4:10 (ICB)

GOD'S LOVE FOR ME IS SPECIAL AND JOYFUL

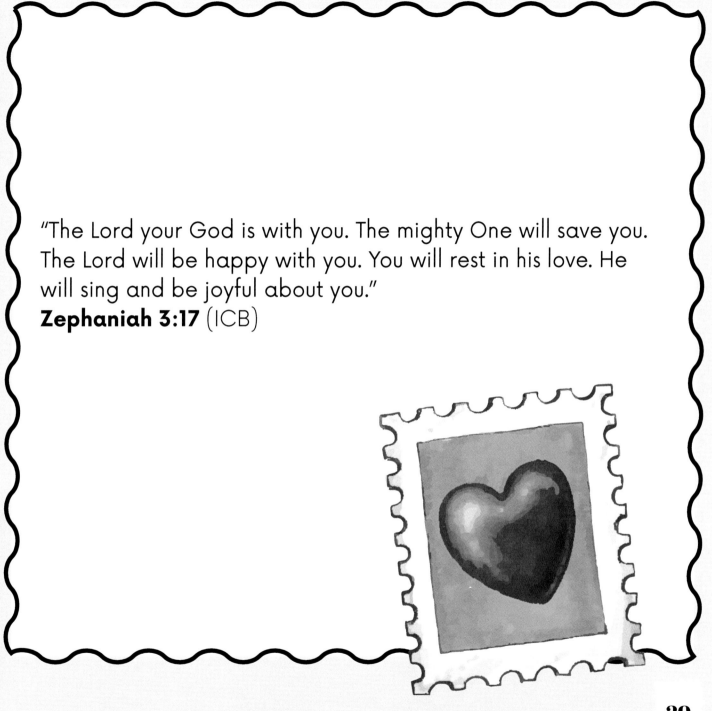

"The Lord your God is with you. The mighty One will save you. The Lord will be happy with you. You will rest in his love. He will sing and be joyful about you."
Zephaniah 3:17 (ICB)

GOD'S LOVE FOR ME NEVER ENDS

"And from far away the Lord appeared to his people. He said, 'I love you people with a love that will last forever. I became your friend because of my love and kindness.'"
Jeremiah 33:1 (ICB)

I AM LOVED BY GOD

GOD LOVES ME!

Section
three

I AM CHOSEN BY GOD

GOD CHOSE ME!

GOD HAS KNOWN ME FOREVER!

"Before I made you in your mother's womb, I chose you. Before you were born, I set you apart for a special work. I appointed you as a prophet to the nations."
Jeremiah 1:5 (ICB)

GOD PICKED ME FROM THE BEGINNING.

"In Christ, he chose us before the world was made. In his love he chose us to be his holy people — people without blame before him."
Ephesians 1:4 (ICB)

GOD HAS SPECIAL PLANS FOR ME!

"'I say this because I know what I have planned for you,' says the Lord. 'I have good plans for you. I don't plan to hurt you. I plan to give you hope and a good future.'"
Jeremiah 29:11 (ICB)

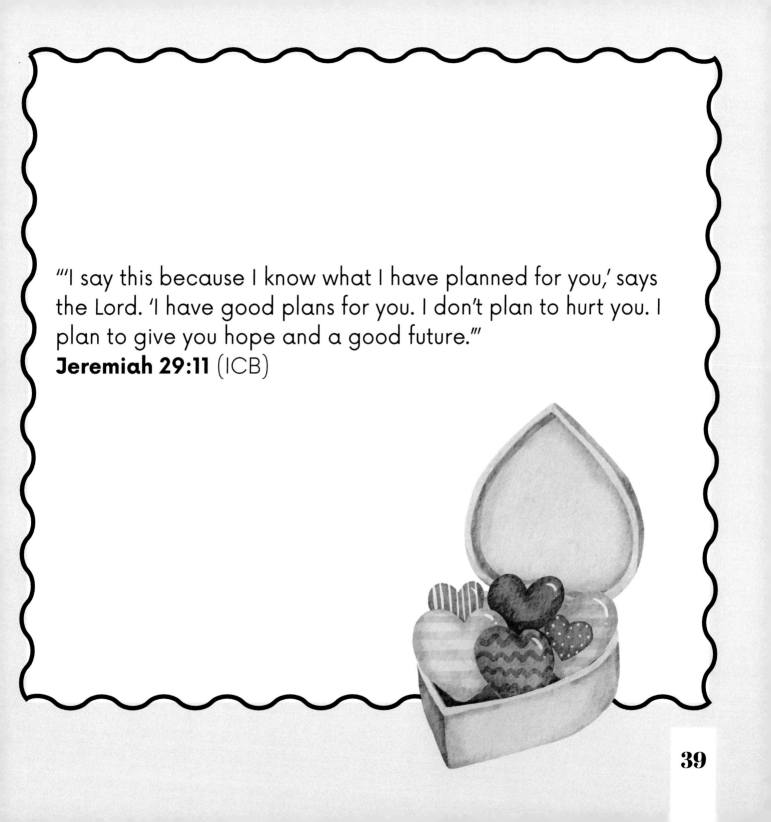

GOD HAS SPECIALLY PICKED ME!

"You did not choose me; I chose you. And I gave you this work, to go and produce fruit. I want you to produce fruit that will last. Then the Father will give you anything you ask for in my name."
John 15:16 (ICB)

GOD HAS CHOSEN ME AS HIS HOLY, PRIESTLY, LIGHT!

I am God's holy child.

I am God's priestly leader.

I am God's light-bearer.

"But you are a chosen people. You are the King's priests. You are a holy nation. You are a nation that belongs to God alone. God chose you to tell about the wonderful things he has done. He called you out of darkness into his wonderful light."
1 Peter 2:9 (ICB)

I AM GOD'S SPECIALLY-CHOSEN REWARD!

"Children are a gift from the Lord. Babies are a reward."
Psalm 127:3 (ICB)

I AM CHOSEN TO BE JUST LIKE GOD!

1   I am known by God.

2   I am chosen by God.

3   I am chosen to be like God

4   Jesus is my brother.

5   Jesus is my example of how to live for God.

"God knew them before he made the world. And God chose them to be like his Son. Then Jesus would be the firstborn of many brothers."
Romans 8:29 (ICB)

SECTION
Four

I AM VICTORIOUS IN GOD!

VICTORY IS MINE!

GOD ALWAYS WANTS VICTORY FOR ME!

"Obey everything that the Lord commands. Follow the commands he has given us. Obey all his laws, and do what he told us. Obey what is written in the teachings of Moses. If you do these things, you will be successful in all you do and wherever you go."
1 Kings 2:3 (ICB)

GOD IS ALWAYS WITH ME TO ENSURE MY VICTORY!

"Teach them to obey everything that I have told you. You can be sure that I will be with you always. I will continue with you until the end of the world."
Matthew 28:20 (ICB)

#1

GOD'S PROMISE
TO BE WITH ME
GIVES ME COURAGE
FOR MY VICTORY.

"Remember that I commanded you to be strong and brave. So don't be afraid. The Lord your God will be with you everywhere you go."
Joshua 1:9 (ICB)

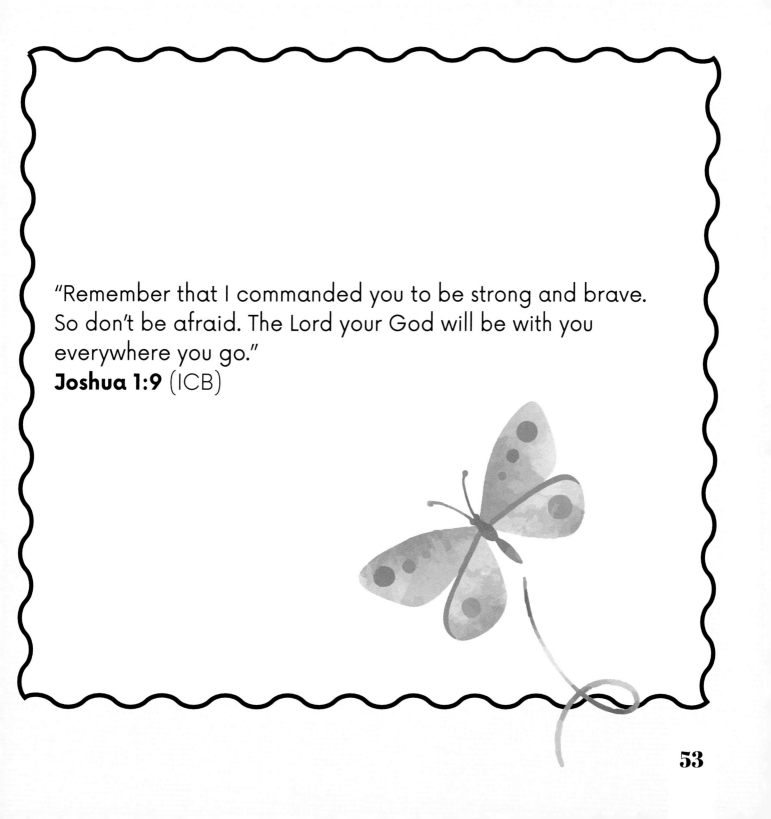

GOD GIVES ME
VICTORY AND
MAKES ALL THINGS
GOOD IN MY LIFE.

"We know that in everything God works for the good of those who love him. They are the people God called, because that was his plan."
Romans 8:28 (ICB)

GOD'S LOVE KEEPS ME VICTORIOUS!

"But in all these things we have full victory through God who showed his love for us."
Romans 8:37 (ICB)

GOD GIVES ME VICTORY POWER AND DOES MORE THAN I CAN DREAM!

"With God's power working in us, God can do much, much more than anything we can ask or think of."
Ephesians 3:20 (ICB)

MY VICTORY IN GOD IS THROUGH JESUS!

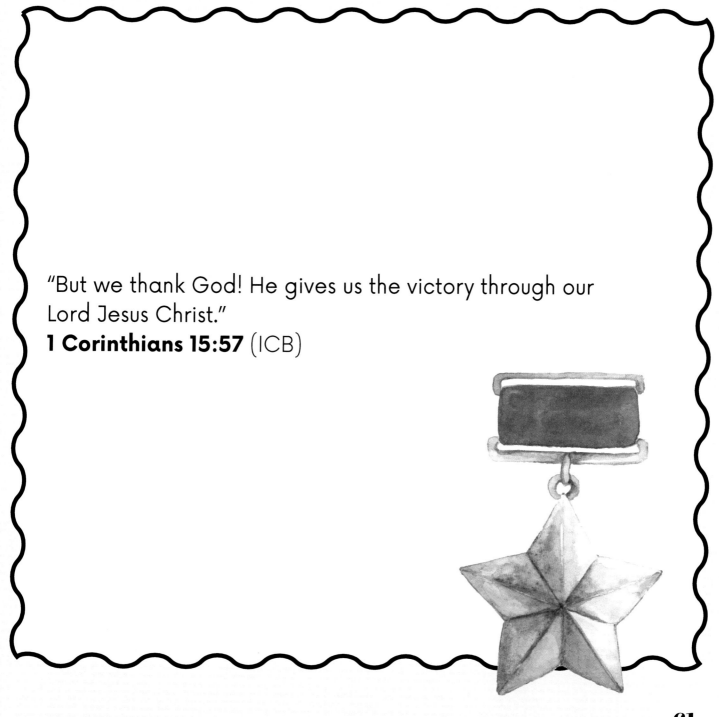

"But we thank God! He gives us the victory through our Lord Jesus Christ."
1 Corinthians 15:57 (ICB)

I AM VICTORIOUS in GOD!

SECTION
Five

I AM PROVIDED FOR BY GOD!

PROMISES

GOD'S PROMISES PROVIDES GREAT BLESSINGS FOR ME AND MY FAMILY!

"May the Lord give you many children. And may he give them children also. May the Lord bless you. He made heaven and earth."
Psalm 115:14-15 (ICB)

GOD PROVIDES ALL I NEED WHEN I FOLLOW HIM.

"The thing you should want most is God's kingdom and doing what God wants. Then all these other things you need will be given to you."
Matthew 6:33 (ICB)

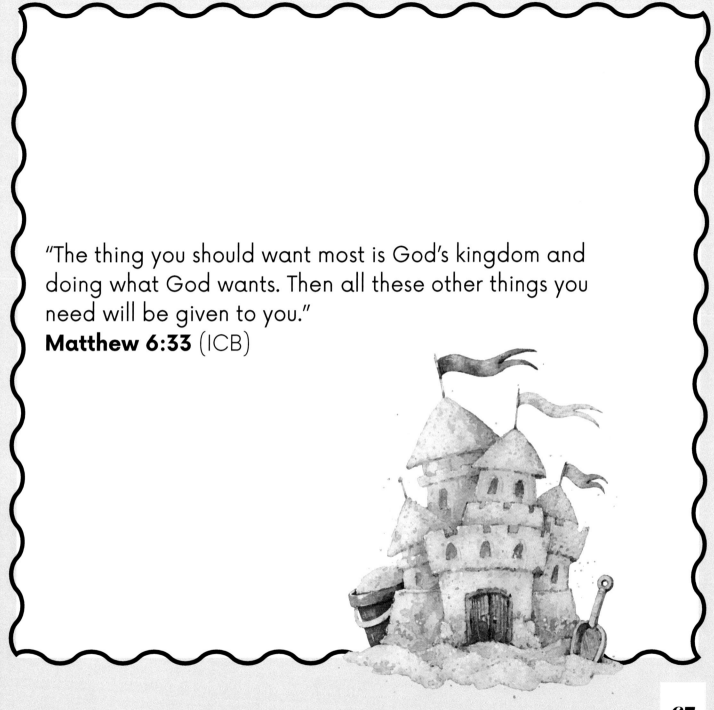

GOD PROVIDES ALL I NEED THROUGH JESUS.

"My God will use his wonderful riches in Christ Jesus to give you everything you need."
Philippians 4:19 (ICB)

THE END IS NOT THE END

While we have reached the end of these affirmations, this is NOT the end. This is only the beginning of the precious promises of God found for us who have been adopted into the family of God through Jesus. Every promise of God belongs to us, His children. Use this book again and again.

Share the good news with others telling them what God says about us. Go to the Bible and find the other precious promises of God: read them, meditate on them, repeat them out loud, listen to them, allow them to get into your heart, mind, and soul so you live them out every day.

Let them empower you to believe and receive everything God says about you! Affirm your greatness; realize your destiny and go forth like Joshua and Jesus in good success!

SALVATION AND RESTORATION PRAYER

If you have not yet joined our family, the family of God, you are invited! God loves and cherishes us more than we know. Come join us in our forever family and choose to love and trust the God of the universe who adores you!

I encourage you to go to God in prayer with your own words and ask to join the family. However, if you need help with the words to say, here are some to get you started.

PRAYER:

Father God, thank You for loving me so much that you sent Jesus to live a life of example for me and to die for sin that separated us. I believe Your Word.

Jesus gives me the right to be adopted into your family just as if I had never sinned and is alive forever praying for me and answering my prayers.

I believe Jesus sent Holy Spirit to give me the power, comfort, and strength to do Your work. I thank You for all you have given me. Please help me to use every gift You give me to be a blessing to others.

I pray in Jesus's name. Amen!

WELCOME!

Welcome to the family of God. God loves you and will never stop! We love you and bless you in Jesus's name.

Made in the USA
Middletown, DE
10 October 2023

40546458R00051